CONTENTS

"Prayer above all recognizes the sovereignty of God - that He is the One who can accomplish far more than we can ask or imagine. I commend this sensitive and much needed prayer guide and Elam's vision to share God's hope with Iranians worldwide."
Ravi Zacharias, author and speaker

"Iran has been on my heart and in my prayers for over 50 years. I only wish in my early days that I could have had such a relevant powerful prayer presentation as this. It needs to be flooded out across the world and for that to happen we need your help."
George Verwer, founder of Operation Mobilisation

"Iran 30 is an important initiative at a critical moment in the history of the Iranian people. I wholeheartedly commend it to you."
Pete Greig, 24-7 Prayer & Alpha International, Director of Prayer

"The Iranian church is alive and well... they need our intercession."
Stuart and Jill Briscoe, Telling the Truth

THANK YOU FOR PRAYING FOR IRAN

Dear Christian Friend,

I want to thank you for setting aside time to pray for my country, Iran. As you'll discover, the Iranian church is growing. Before the 1979 revolution hardly any Muslims became Christians; now Iranians are the most open people in the Islamic world to the Gospel.

Thousands have come to faith in Christ, and thousands more want to. With prayer, we can see explosive church growth in Iran, which will impact all of the Muslim Middle East.

Church growth always brings opposition and Iran is no exception. There is a real possibility that the present intimidation Christians suffer will turn into severe persecution.

I am in constant touch with many Christians in Iran: above all they ask for prayer. So on their behalf – a sincere thank you.

Your prayers will change things.

Yours in His grace,

Sam Yeghnazar
Director, Elam Ministries

Seeing the people, He felt
compassion for them...

Matthew 9:36

Day 1   Iran, land of open hearts

On this first day let us lift the whole nation of Iran before the living God who answers prayer:

A nation whose history stretches back 2,500 years and whose kings served God's people when they were suffering in exile in Bible times.

A nation that ended 25 centuries of monarchy in 1979 and brought in a revolutionary Islamic regime.

A nation of 66 million people, most of them young and well educated. Two thirds of the people are under 30 and 80% of the population are literate.

A nation that geographically is the largest in the Middle East, with vast reserves of oil and gas.

A nation whose government opposes Christianity: Bibles are banned; evangelism is illegal; converts could face the death sentence.

But also a nation whose disillusioned people have become the most open Muslims in the world to the Gospel.

And a nation where the church is growing faster than at any other time since the arrival of Islam in the 7th century.

PRAY FOR IRAN

◆ *For churches to be planted in thousands of towns and villages.*

◆ *For brave servants to be raised up to lead the church.*

◆ *For the enemies of the church to be restrained.*

IRAN, IN THE HEART OF THE MUSLIM WORLD

Russia

Georgia

Uzbekistan

Armenia Azerbaijan

Turkmenistan

Tajikistan

ria

◆
Tabriz

◆ Tehran

◆ Mashad

Afghanistan

Iraq

Iran

◆ Esfahan

Kuwait

◆ Shiraz

Pakistan

Qatar

U.A.E.

Saudi Arabia

Oman

Yemen

Iranians are an Indo-European people.
They speak Persian (Farsi), not Arabic.
90% are Shia Muslim.

SUFFERING, BUT GROWING CHURCH

These are crucial days in the long history of the church in Iran. There is solid evidence both of unprecedented openness to the Gospel and also of church growth; but the church continues to face severe opposition. At least eight Christians have been murdered for their faith, and hundreds imprisoned.

DAY 2 IN PRISON, OFTEN WITHOUT CHARGE

Over fifty Christians were arrested in 2008 for their faith. Possibly the figure is higher. Some were released the same day; others were kept for months. Inside prison, apart from grim living conditions, there is the risk of solitary confinement, or worse, and worrying uncertainty.

Arrested in May 2008, Mahmood Azad and Arash Basirat were kept in solitary confinement. On July 15th they were put in a cell together. Neither of them had been charged. In early August they came before a Revolutionary Court and were accused of 'apostasy', putting them potentially on death row. But on September 23rd they were released.

The arrest of Christians has continued in 2009. This has two aims. One is to get more information about the house churches, so computers and mobile phones are confiscated and prisoners are constantly questioned. The other aim is to intimidate. With these arrests they hope to frighten active Christians so either they will lie low or leave the country.

PRAY FOR THE PERSECUTED

◆ *For the presence of the Holy Spirit to be with all who are arrested for their faith.*

◆ *For the families of the prisoners.*

◆ *For intimidation of the church to stop.*

Rev. Arastoo Sayyah
- Apostate from Islam
- Priest Anglican Church, Shiraz
- Throat cut February 1979

Bahram Dehqani
- Son of Anglican 'apostate' bishop
- Shot dead May 1980
- Murderers unknown

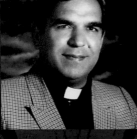

Rev. Hussein Soodmand
- Apostate from Islam
- Assemblies of God Pastor, Mashad
- Hanged in prison December 1990

Bishop Haik Hovsepian-Mehr
- Campaigner for religious freedom
- Superintendent AOG Churches
- Stabbed to death January 1994
- Murderers unknown

DAY 3 MARTYRS, THE ULTIMATE PRICE

Eight Christian leaders have been murdered in Iran since 1979 because of their witness. Their martyrdoms underline the need to pray against the Islamic law of apostasy that demands the death sentence for any male apostate from Islam, and life imprisonment for women. Most members of the growing house churches are threatened by this law.

Rev. Tateos Michaelian
- Campaigner for religious freedom
- Pastor Presbyterian Church, Tehran
- Shot dead June 1994
- Murderers unknown

Mehdi Dibaj
- Apostate from Islam
- Evangelist
- Shot dead June 1994
- Murderers unknown

Mohammad Yusefi
- Apostate from Islam
- Pastor of Sari churches
- Hanged in forest September 1996
- Murderers unknown

Ghorban Tourani
- Apostate from Islam
- House Church leader
- Stabbed to death November 2005
- Murderers unknown

PRAY FOR THE MARTYRS' LEGACY

◆ *For it to inspire Christians to preach boldly, despite the risk of being killed.*

◆ *For it to set an example for new believers.*

◆ *For it to comfort the families of the martyrs.*

Day 4 Meeting in homes, it's safer

In 1996, after the murder of Muslim convert pastor Mohammad Yusefi, Christian leaders decided the future of the church had to be underground. The government would never allow an evangelical church to grow in great numbers.

Though church buildings stayed open, the main work focused on house churches, which have flourished. Nobody knows exactly how many groups there are, but a cautious estimate would be several hundred in ten or more networks. This means that every day believers are meeting together somewhere in Iran.

The house church Christians are passionate evangelists, but they need to be cautious about security. Seekers are first met in a public place, and they are not introduced to a house church until the leaders are completely sure they are genuine. Infiltrators are a constant threat.

For the new believer the invitation to a house group meeting, rather than to a conspicuous church building, is welcome.

Whether there is singing or not depends on the neighbors. The meeting has to appear like a social gathering and to be quiet so not to arouse the suspicions of neighbors. For the same reason, the meeting place keeps on changing.

PRAY FOR HOUSE CHURCHES

◆ *For hundreds of house church meetings today in Iran. Pray they will multiply.*

◆ *For constant wisdom so neighbors do not report on the house churches.*

◆ *Against infiltrators.*

DAY 5 CHURCH IN BUILDINGS, BE WARY

The government claims there is religious freedom and allows some church buildings to exist. Ethnic groups, such as Assyrians and Armenians, are given relative freedom, but only because their services are held in their own languages. They are unlikely to convert Iranian Persian-speaking Muslims.

But it is a different story for the Anglican, Presbyterian, and Assemblies of God churches, which were legally established before the 1979 revolution. Altogether they have less than ten legally recognized Persian-speaking churches in the country. These churches have services in Persian and by doing so are, by definition, seeking to convert Iranian Muslims who only speak Persian.

They face many restrictions and must be very wary. At every service there are infiltrators; pastors must report to the government; and they and other members have their phones tapped. In some cities such as Kerman, the authorities have closed down their churches. In Mashad they hanged the Assemblies of God pastor and later shut the church.

Despite the government's efforts to suffocate these churches, they are still an important witness for Christ.

PRAY FOR ESTABLISHED CHURCHES

◆ *For brave discernment for all in leadership.*

◆ *For true courage when dealing with seekers.*

◆ *For the worship to rise above fear.*

DAY 6 EVANGELISM, HAPPENS EVERY DAY

Iranian Christians read the Bible and try to do what it tells them. So they take their responsibility to evangelize seriously in spite of the real risks they face. They have especially taken Acts 13:1-3 to heart where there is first prayer and fasting – then evangelism.

There are many remarkable testimonies that can only be described as 'divine appointments'. Christians have witnessed to seekers on religious marches; they have found themselves on buses showing films about Christ; they have led people to faith in taxis; they have witnessed successfully to women who work on the street. It is through this Holy Spirit led evangelism that new fellowships are planted.

Despite being constantly watched, the established churches are also active in sharing the Gospel. Even if informants are sitting in the services, the full Gospel is preached and guests are invited to repent. Sometimes people get up from their seats and come to the front of the church even before the sermon has finished.

On the streets people are remarkably open. The wife of one church leader gave out many thousands of copies of the 'Jesus Film' based on the Gospel of Luke - only two people refused them.

PRAY FOR EVANGELISM

◆ **For fervent evangelism to continue.**

◆ **For protection of evangelists.**

◆ **For more divine appointments.**

DAY 7   DISCIPLESHIP, DEFINITELY DIFFICULT

One church planter shares: *"Many people are coming to Christ, but the challenge is to make them deep in the Lord and in His Word."*

First there is the security challenge, so discipleship has to be done cautiously – though new believers are encouraged to be a witness.

Secondly, there is the task of 'renewing the mind' and dealing with the many false teachings ingrained from their previous religion. Much time is spent on the basics, especially the Trinity.

Thirdly, discipleship is difficult because leaders have often only been Christians themselves for a short time. These 'older' Christians try their best, but are hampered as they sometimes don't have Scriptures or books to give to their disciples.

Fourthly, many believers come from very broken backgrounds, and need a lot of time.

Finally, there are many isolated believers. For them, growing as followers of Christ is especially difficult and they need special prayer covering.

PRAY FOR DISCIPLESHIP

◆ *For those who are teaching, that they have the wisdom to impart truth.*

◆ *For new believers to grow as disciples.*

◆ *For isolated Christians.*

Day 8 Jobs, scarce for Christians

When Muslims become Christians, they can easily lose their jobs because of their new faith. The economy is dominated by the Islamic government. From the biggest factories to the smallest farms, bureaucrats are in the background. Many Christian converts tread wisely and sometimes manage to keep their job. But often word gets out and they are forced to resign, or they are fired. Islamic employers usually will not tolerate 'apostates'. Setting up their own businesses is also fraught with danger, as acquiring the necessary paper work means dealing with the state.

Though Iran's ethnic minority Christians, the Assyrians and Armenians, do not face the same level of intimidation, they have still found employment and business very challenging. The best jobs are always reserved for Muslims.

The business world doesn't operate on a level playing-field either. It is dominated by Islamic 'charities' that fund businesses using the massive income generated from religious shrines and mosques. At every stage 'insiders' are given preferential treatment.

This inequality impacts everyone, but especially minorities like Christians. To properly support their family some conclude their only choice is to leave the country.

PRAY FOR JOBS

◆ *Against discrimination and for Christians to find favor with their employers.*

◆ *For Christians to devise ingenious ways of creating businesses and providing employment.*

◆ *For Christians to be a good example at work.*

SOCIETY STRESSED

There is much to be admired in Iranian society: a strong emphasis on family; respect for the old; and outright rejection of Hollywood morality.

Yet underneath the dignified exterior there lurks drug addiction, depression, prostitution, and a rising divorce rate.

We need to pray that those suffering in a stressed society would find His peace.

Day 9   Family, Worrying Trends

In the midst of all Iran's storms, the strength of the family has remained. Iranians are renowned for their exuberant hospitality, and families and friends spend much time enjoying each other's company at large parties or, in the summer, at picnics in the park.

But there are worrying trends tearing at the fabric of families. Divorce is on the increase and is now about 13%, though there are many more unhappy marriages. Because of Islamic divorce law, children usually end up in the father's custody - so many mothers choose to stay in a difficult marriage to raise their children.

With low wages, high unemployment and inflation, families live under severe financial pressure. Fathers are often absent from home as they have to work in two or three jobs to make ends meet. Millions of young Iranians are not getting married because they simply cannot afford to do so. This stress also leads many to seek a better life abroad and so families are separated from each other.

There are official reports of a dramatic increase in promiscuity, which leaves behind its usual miserable trail of abortions and broken hearts. Though the vast majority of Iranians frown on polygamy, the Shia faith allows men four wives. It also permits 'temporary marriage', that can be for just a few hours. Neither a new nor temporary wife helps family harmony.

PRAY FOR FAMILIES

◆ *For many entire households to be saved.*

◆ *For strong family life in Iran.*

◆ *Against promiscuity and abortions.*

Day 10 The Economy,
A cause for anger

Iran should have a very successful economy. It holds 10% of the world's crude oil reserves, and in terms of natural gas is second only to Russia.

And yet Iran today has a poor economic record. Inflation has been over 20% and unemployment is around 15%. This figure will rise as nearly one million enter the job market each year.

The mismanagement of the economy, especially in the vast public sector, is causing intense anger. Salaries are not raised according to inflation and sometimes are not even paid on time. In recent years bus drivers and teachers have gone on strike over this. The protests ended with the organizers being jailed.

In the private sector there is little competition, which means high prices.

This poor economic record forces many breadwinners to take on a second job, which is usually low paid. Iranians' economic struggle is made worse when they see how other countries with fewer natural resources enjoy a better life.

Sometimes they take their frustration to the streets, as when gas was first rationed due to the lack of refineries.

PRAY FOR THE ECONOMY

- *For Iranians to discover their true riches in Christ.*
- *For families who are living below the poverty line.*
- *For better management of the economy.*

MULLAHS,
MEN UNDER PRESSURE

About 200,000 mullahs work in over 50,000 mosques and Islamic seminaries in Iran. They have a lot of influence but they are under pressure because of people's intense frustration with the religious regime.

Some mullahs are no doubt motivated by political power, but many are ordinary men who want to please God and serve their communities. As well as their ceremonial duties, they deal with local disputes, give support and offer words of wisdom.

They lead the Friday prayers; deliver sermons; officiate at weddings and funerals; and they are very active in numerous Muslim schools and charities. All of this means they have tremendous influence, particularly in the small towns and villages.

Many of these mullahs can become 'obedient to the faith'. Like religious men in Paul's day, they 'are zealous for God, but their zeal is not based on knowledge' (Romans 10:2). Already some mullahs have turned to Christ and some church planters in Iran today became Christians while studying in Islamic seminaries.

PRAY FOR MULLAHS

◆ *That many mullahs will receive Christ and preach the Gospel.*

◆ *That they will meet and be impacted by the lives and testimonies of Christians.*

◆ *For students in Islamic seminaries to find Christ.*

DAY 12 WOMEN, LEGALLY DEVALUED

Iranian women, renowned for their strength of character, are active in nearly every area of life. From family to education and even politics, women make their mark.

However, they face discrimination at every turn. While strict dress regulations irritate some women, their legal status is offensive. For example:

- A woman's testimony in court is worth half that of a man's.
- In cases where blood money is demanded, say after a fatal accident, a woman's worth is half that of a man's.
- A man can have four wives and as many temporary ones as he wants.
- In divorce, a man can initiate proceedings for many reasons. There are limited exceptions where women can start the process.

This injustice, coupled with a low view of the value of women, often leads to intense abuse within society. And when they suffer, their religion offers no protection. This partially explains the special interest women have for Jesus Christ who shows them such radical respect. 60% of new believers in Iran are women and they are passionate Christians: eager for more Bible teaching.

PRAY FOR WOMEN

◆ *For more women to follow Jesus.*

◆ *For the dignity that Christianity gives women to be seen in the nation.*

◆ *For their legal position to be improved.*

DAY 13   YOUTH, WANTING FREEDOM

About 15 million out of the 66 million people in Iran are under 15. Two thirds of the population is under 30. And these millions switch off when bearded religious leaders talk about their revolution. Their minds are not on the past but on the future. And they have two major frustrations.

First, they want more social and intellectual freedom. They are tired of being told what they should wear, watch or read.

Secondly, they want meaningful jobs. Nearly one million enter the labor market every year. The government uses oil money to create work, but not enough.

For the church, this is an extraordinary opportunity. Millions of young Iranians have time to browse the Internet and watch satellite TV where they can hear about Jesus.

This curiosity has led many to look for a New Testament. When they find one, some finish it in a matter of days.

House churches are often full of young people, and many church leaders and planters are under 25.

PRAY FOR YOUTH

◆ *For more youth to come to faith in Christ and to find God's purpose for their lives.*

◆ *For young Christians to be a powerful witness.*

◆ *For more ministries to reach the youth.*

نفرین سیاه را یاسخ گفتند

DAY 14　　　DRUGS, TOO MANY

Forget dress restrictions or even unemployment: the open wound across Iran is drug addiction.

Whatever the number of addicts – the government says one million, others say four million – the pain is etched on the face of the user, their shame and sickness shared by the family. Some blame unemployment, but the real reason is that heroin is cheap and plentiful.

Pouring in from neighboring Afghanistan, government officials are fighting a hard war against the traffickers. They have had some success. Figures show nearly 70% of all heroin confiscated worldwide is seized in Iran.

This success comes with a price: since the revolution, 3,600 border guards have been killed in shoot-outs with the drug barons.

All around the world, Christians have proved that they run the best rehabilitation centers. Their methods work. Iran is no exception. Many individuals have been delivered and have testified openly to the power of Christ. Their witness wins many.

PRAY FOR DRUG ADDICTS

◆ *For addicts and their families to know that Christ can set them free.*

◆ *For Christians to minister in powerful but wise ways to bring freedom to addicts.*

◆ *For government officials bravely fighting drug barons on the Iran- Afghan border.*

Ali's story: 'I killed my brother'

Until he became a teenager, Ali was like any other boy on the block in down town Tehran. Then he became a heroin addict. His parents arranged for him to get married, hoping this would cure him. It didn't and the marriage collapsed. Worse was to happen. Ali had drawn his younger brother, Farhad, into the world of drug addiction.

One cold winter day Farhad did not come back home. Ali went out looking for him, and found him lying in the street. He was dead. He had taken an overdose. Standing there Ali felt heaven and earth screaming around him as he confessed with loud cries, 'I have killed my brother!' The only answer to his guilt was to take more drugs. In fact he wanted to overdose and die. He went to his favorite haunt, determined to do this. And while sitting there a young girl, a complete stranger, came up to him and simply told him that God loved him and gave him a New Testament. Ali did not overdose and later managed to read about the Man who freed those with legions of demons. He called to Jesus Christ and was saved – from the searing guilt of his brother's death, and from bondage to heroin.

Today he serves Christ in Iran.

DAY 15   DEPRESSION, TOO COMMON

The stress and pressures of life have caused an epidemic of depression. Nobody knows the exact figures. Some reports say it is up to 20% of the population, and others say over 70% of young people, especially girls, are afflicted.

There is no shortage of pundits suggesting reasons: unemployment, drugs, long working hours, family stress, intrusive religious policies, and discriminatory legislation. The list is endless. But there is a desperate shortage of answers. Many sufferers turn to anti-depressants.

Though tragic, this situation has meant that many are searching for happiness and that attracts them to Christianity. Often the first thing Muslim enquirers notice when they visit Christian meetings is the joy and exuberance in the worship.

House church leaders dealing with Christians suffering from depression need special wisdom and training.

PRAY FOR THE DEPRESSED

◆ **For the chronically depressed, that they will find peace.**

◆ **For Christians to be equipped to minister to the depressed.**

◆ **For all who care for them – families, doctors, and nurses.**

REACHING IRAN

What does it take to reach a country like Iran?

Courageous and trained leaders; the Word of God; inspiring books; attractive websites and satellite TV programs – and above all, fervent prayer.

Day 16   Leaders, more please

Courageous men and women have poured out their lives for the Gospel, but the reality is there are far too few trained leaders serving in Iran.

While there are many believers who passionately want to serve, the government does not allow Bible schools and church training programs. Therefore, almost all leadership training for the church has to happen outside the country and this is a major challenge.

There are some strong programs in place, including a degree level course, a three-month church planting course, conferences and correspondence courses. These have been effective – wherever properly trained leaders are serving, the church is growing.

But with the church growing rapidly, there is an acute need for programs inside the country to train large numbers of emerging leaders. Iran's church needs more church planters, evangelists and pastors to reap the harvest, as well as anointed theologians who can defend Christian truth and protect the church from heresy.

PRAY FOR MORE LEADERS

◆ *For existing programs to train more godly leaders.*

◆ *For the Lord to provide ways for leadership programs to start inside Iran.*

◆ *For existing leaders – for protection, anointing and wisdom.*

DAY 17 SCRIPTURE, CHANGES NATIONS

Millions of people want to read the Christian Scriptures, but printing and importing the Bible is strictly illegal. One new convert was so desperate she made her own 'Bible' by writing down verses quoted on satellite TV; others have printed out the whole New Testament from the net.

Christians have sent in hundreds of thousands of Scriptures but in a country of 66 million, demand dwarfs supply. The brave distributors, who risk their lives, always want more. They say that 95% receive the New Testament with joy.

In the 1980s, one million Bibles were sent to China and today the Chinese church is the largest in the world. The same can happen in Iran. Church leaders want at least a million New Testaments distributed as soon as possible.

PRAY FOR SCRIPTURES

◆ *For the goal to print and distribute one million New Testaments in Iran by the end of 2013.*

◆ *For protection and wisdom for all who distribute Scriptures.*

◆ *For on-going Bible translation projects.*

DAY 18 BOOKS, FAMINE CONDITIONS

It is illegal for the church to print or sell Persian Christian books. One would-be publisher was told by a government officer that anyone producing Christian literature deserved to be executed.

So Christian books are very scarce. Some brave believers photocopy material, but this is dangerous. Most books have to be brought into Iran by smugglers. Once available, demand far outstrips supply. One church leader obtained 2,500 books and they all went in two weeks.

As well as supply problems, there is also a severe lack of good Christian literature in Persian. While the Arab world has over 10,000 titles to choose from, Iran has less than 400, many of which are old and out of date. There is a shortage of theological books, commentaries, and for children the situation is desperate: there are less than twenty titles.

PRAY FOR LITERATURE

◆ *For those involved in the translation and production of books.*

◆ *For more books to be authored by Iranian Christians.*

◆ *For widespread distribution, and lives to be changed.*

DAY 19 INTERNET, GREAT SUPPORT

Iran has an estimated 23 million Internet users who spend a lot of time surfing the net. And Iranians love blogging: Persian ranks as the third most common blogging language, after English and Mandarin.

Every week thousands access Christian websites to read and learn about the faith. It is quite common to hear converts refer to the Internet when they give their testimonies. One of the most courageous church planters became a Christian through the Internet in 2005 and by the end of 2008 had planted four churches.

For many isolated believers the Internet is their only means of finding Bible material, especially because Christian literature is so scarce. They can print Scriptures, books, and articles they would otherwise never get.

For house churches, Christian websites provide material to help with their meetings. And for radio and TV ministries they are vital for follow up.

PRAY FOR THE INTERNET

- ◆ *For seekers to find Christ as they surf the net.*
- ◆ *For Christians and house churches to be strengthened by material on the net.*
- ◆ *For Persian Christian websites to have wider exposure in Iran.*

AMIR'S STORY: WANTS PORN, FINDS CHRIST

Amir, a seventeen year old boy from Shiraz, got into the habit of browsing sleazy sites at an Internet café. One day he typed 'sex' into the search engine and a video came up In Persian called 'Pornography'. He clicked on this and sat back to watch.

But instead this was a Christian program, bluntly pointing out how pornography damages people's integrity. Amir was already feeling guilty about his habit, so kept on watching. There was a moving testimony about a man who nearly destroyed his marriage because of porn, and then the two presenters shared how Jesus Christ still loves us, even when we have sinned sexually. This amazed him. He thought God would hate him because of his lust.

He took down the number given on the program and a few days later phoned up the TV station's office... it was, of course, outside Iran, so the call cost. But it was worth it. Amir talked for a long time with the counselor and was more than ready to give his life to Christ at the end of the conversation.

DAY 20   SATELLITE TV, HUGE IMPACT

Satellite TV has emerged as perhaps the most effective way of reaching millions with the Gospel. Despite the government ban, dishes are very popular and there are an estimated 28 million who watch satellite TV.

In recent years several ministries have worked to produce Persian Christian programs that are broadcast into the country from abroad. There is plenty of anecdotal evidence that significant numbers watch Christian programs.

Hundreds of phone calls and emails are received each week as people respond and ask questions or request Bibles and other Christian materials. Several house churches have been established as a result of TV ministry.

As well as its evangelistic impact, TV provides a great source of teaching and encouragement for many Christians. It is reported that some fellowships meet around the TV as part of their weekly gatherings.

PRAY FOR SATELLITE TV

◆ **For the ministries that produce Christian programs for Iran.**

◆ **For more high quality programs to be made.**

◆ **For isolated Christians and house churches who rely on Christian TV.**

DAY 21   DVDS, NICE AND LIGHT

Most households have a DVD player, and because DVDs are nice and light they can easily be sent into the country and distributed. You can fit about 1,000 DVDs into one ordinary suitcase.

The 'Jesus Film', based on the Gospel of Luke, has been distributed widely and has helped hundreds, if not thousands, come to repentance. In 2008, 50,000 copies were made and more are already needed.

Another important DVD is 'Magdalena – Released from Shame', based on the story of Mary Magdalene, which is especially popular among women.

For children there is great demand for the 'Story Keepers' cartoon series which is being distributed and is much loved. Some kids watch the DVD over 20 times a week!

These and other DVDs are having a major evangelistic impact.

DVDs are also excellent for bringing good Bible teaching to churches.

PRAY FOR DVDs

◆ *For millions of Christian DVDs to flood Iran.*

◆ *For protection for suppliers and distributors.*

◆ *For follow up for those who respond.*

DAY 22   DIASPORA CHRISTIANS, ALWAYS VISITING

The Islamic revolution has driven four million Iranians abroad where, more than any other group of immigrants from the Middle East, they have been turning to Christ. In Europe there are fellowships in every major country, and in America there are churches in at least twenty-two states. There are also thousands of Iranians who have joined the national churches of their host countries.

These Christians are very significant for Iran. They are in constant contact with their loved ones back home, and often they get an opportunity to visit the country and share their new faith. There are reports of whole families who have become Christians through their witness.

Some of these Christians also play a major role in sending books and New Testaments; producing satellite TV programs; hosting evangelistic web sites; and when necessary, playing a crucial role in campaigning for religious freedom.

PRAY FOR IRANIANS WORLDWIDE

◆ *For Christians as they contact and visit family and friends in Iran.*

◆ *For their role in sending resources and speaking up for the church in Iran.*

◆ *For more national churches to reach out to Iranians in their midst.*

INFLUENTIAL INSTITUTIONS

The Bible is clear: Christians are to pray for those in authority, whoever they are. And that includes all the institutions the rulers rely on – the judiciary, the military, the commercial leaders and the media.

Our prayers for these institutions can make a massive difference to the lives of millions of ordinary Iranians.

DAY 23 SHIA RULERS, NEED PRAYER

'I urge, then, first of all, that requests, prayers, intercession and thanksgiving be made for everyone - for kings and all those in authority...' (1 Timothy 2:1-2)

Though the rulers of Iran have not been friends of the church, we should still pray for them as they rule over 66 million people. Their decisions matter at home - and in the world. It will be their deliberations that impact the outcome of Iran's ambition to develop a nuclear capacity. The key positions in the government are:

- Supreme Leader
- President
- Chairman of the Assembly of Experts
- Speaker of Parliament
- Chairman of the Guardian Council
- Head of Judiciary
- Head of National Security Council.

Visit **iran30.org** to pray for the current leaders by name.

Pray also for thousands of regional leaders who impact Christians in their communities.

PRAY FOR THE GOVERNMENT

◆ *That the Holy Spirit will lead them to Christ.*

◆ *That God will influence their decisions.*

◆ *For a peaceful resolution to the nuclear issue.*

HOW IRAN IS GOVERNED*

ELECTED INSTITUTIONS →   ← **UNELECTED INSTITUTIONS**

ELECTORATE
All over 16 can vote.

PRESIDENT
Though elected for a four year term, the President has to be vetted by the Guardian Council and confirmed by the Supreme Leader.

THE SUPREME LEADER
He is an agent of Shia Islam and holds supreme power on the basis that he can best interpret Islamic law. He appoints six members of the Guardian Council, all the members of the Expediency Council, the heads of the armed forces and judiciary, the Friday prayer leaders and the directors of TV and Radio.

THE CABINET
The Cabinet is chosen by the President, but ministers must be approved by Parliament. As the Supreme Leader is actively involved in defence, security, and foreign policy, ministers must be able to work with his office.

ARMED FORCES
With at least half a million in active service in both the regular and revolutionary forces, and twenty million available if needed, Iran's armed forces are by far the largest in the Middle East. The Supreme Leader is the commander in chief.

HEAD OF JUDICIARY
Appointed by the Supreme Leader, the incumbent's role is to uphold revolutionary values through the judiciary. It is his courts that Christians find themselves in when arrested for practising their faith.

PARLIAMENT
The 290 MPs elected for four years are vetted by the Guardian Council, as is all the legislation they pass.

EXPEDIENCY COUNCIL
This small advisory body's role is to settle disputes between Parliament and the Guardian Council. All members are appointed by the Supreme Leader.

THE ASSEMBLY OF EXPERTS
This 86 member body is responsible for appointing the Supreme Leader if he dies or resigns, and to dismiss him if he proves incompetent. Members are elected every eight years, all candidates are vetted by the Guardian Council. They meet twice a year.

KEY:
→ Directly appointed
→ Appointed or approved
- → Vets candidates

THE GUARDIAN COUNCIL
Made up of six theologians appointed by the Supreme Leader and six jurists nominated by the judiciary and approved by Parliament. The Guardian Council vets all presidential, parliamentary and Assembly of Expert candidates, and all legislation. Members serve for six years.

Day 24 Military service, every man's duty

Every able-bodied man over 19 must do military service for at least 18 months: women are exempt. About 500,000 ordinary young men serve at any one time. Most join the regular army, but some prefer to serve in the more fanatical Revolutionary Guards.

Military service is the state's opportunity to cement into young men the values of the Islamic revolution. So as well as going to prayers five times a day, there are also compulsory lectures on revolutionary Islam to attend. This means it is very challenging for any Muslim who has become a Christian.

Since the end of the Iran-Iraq war in 1988 when hundreds of thousands of conscripts died, military service has not been arduous. After two months of training, most recruits serve in their own locality. The most dangerous posting is supporting the customs in their fight with Afghan drug smugglers.

However, if an international conflict breaks out over Iran's nuclear program, it is these young men who will pay the price.

PRAY FOR THE MILITARY

◆ *For the protection of all the young men doing military service.*

◆ *That their experience will make them open to Jesus Christ.*

◆ *For Christians doing military service to be as wise as serpents and harmless as doves.*

DAY 25 JUDICIARY, SHADOWY POWERS

There are two judicial systems in Iran, the civil and the revolutionary. Both are Islamic (all secular law was abolished in 1982) and come under the unelected head of the judiciary – accountable to the Supreme Leader.

The civil courts deal with criminal, commercial, and family law; the revolutionary courts with perceived threats to the Islamic regime. Here there are arbitrary arrests and usually defendants have no access to lawyers or a right of appeal. Charges can be as sweeping as 'blasphemy against God' or 'insulting Islam'.

This court system is frightening for all Iranians, but journalists and trade unionists have to be especially wary – as do Christians. For it is to these courts they are brought when arrested by the authorities. And it is in these courts that believers from Muslim backgrounds can be charged with apostasy, which carries the death sentence for men, and life imprisonment for women. Also, believers can be falsely accused of supporting foreign 'Christian' powers.

PRAY FOR THE JUDICIAL SYSTEM

◆ *For the head of the judiciary and all the judges to love justice and mercy.*

◆ *That prisoners will have fair trials.*

◆ *For officials and prisoners to hear the Gospel.*

DAY 26   EDUCATION, MOLDING MINDS

Iran's record in education since the 1979 revolution is good. School is free, and for gifted students higher education is as well. The teacher to pupil ratio (about 1:30) is reasonable; discipline throughout the single sex system is strong, and academic standards are high. Education, then, for most Iranians is a true learning experience.

However the government does not only want to educate: it wants to mold the minds of the young.

So education is very Islamic: a generous amount of the timetable is given to Islamic studies; all the textbooks and teachers are vetted for religious orthodoxy; and failure in the Islamic examinations can seriously impede a student's career. Those in the educational system who fall out of line are swiftly dealt with, especially at the universities.

Despite this indoctrination it is clear from numerous Internet blogs that not all minds have been molded: many question the Islamic creed.

PRAY FOR STUDENTS

◆ *For Christians who have to be very wise in these institutions, especially in their witness.*

◆ *For staff and pupils to hear the Gospel.*

◆ *For wisdom and strength for all the teachers.*

DAY 27   BUSINESS, CAN BE CRONY CAPITALISM

The Islamic Revolution was led by mullahs but financially supported by powerful merchants in the country's bazaars - men notorious for 'creative accounting'. Their opaque ways now influence much of how business is done throughout the economy.

Dubbed 'crony capitalism', their system has made a few insiders fabulously wealthy. Not surprisingly, with most Iranians struggling financially, this has caused intense resentment.

Many associate religion with getting rich, so Christians have an opportunity to show ordinary people by example how Jesus rejected the love of money.

However, being a Christian in the business community is a daunting task as most enterprises are allied with the mosque. Those in business who have turned to Christ need exceptional courage and wisdom.

PRAY FOR BUSINESS

◆ *For revival and transformation in the business world.*

◆ *For fair trade.*

◆ *For business opportunities for Christians.*

DAY 28 MEDIA, TIGHTLY CONTROLLED

Since 1979, the government has controlled all TV, radio, and the newspapers. In the 1990s there was a brief spell under President Khatami when there was some freedom for the printed press. However there was a ferocious backlash from the judiciary leading to the imprisonment of reformist editors and journalists and those days ended.

In this controlled environment there is some discussion between different factions of the conservative elite – but there is no questioning of the basic values upholding the Islamic Republic: the Supreme Leader is never questioned; Shia Islam is the true faith; nuclear power is Iran's undeniable right; the USA is the 'big' Satan; and Israel is the 'crusader' state.

Though Christianity rarely appears in the media, when it does, its treatment is disingenuous. The media gives the impression there is religious freedom for Christians when there isn't. The government has produced TV documentaries, and published booklets and newspaper articles to discredit Christianity.

PRAY FOR THE MEDIA

◆ *Against all propaganda discrediting the Bible and Christianity.*

◆ *For those working in the media to be reached by the Gospel.*

◆ *For protection for journalists who speak up for truth.*

DAY 29 CINEMA, WORLDWIDE SUCCESS

Though cinemas were burned during the Islamic Revolution, the industry has risen from those ashes to have massive influence – in Iran, throughout the Middle East and worldwide. The films that delight the international audiences and win coveted awards tend to be those that verge on the surreal by directors like Kiarostami and Makhmalbaf.

More popular in the Middle East and Iran are the action films. And everyone loves comedies like *Marmulak,* about an escaped thief who pretends to be a mullah, or *Maxx,* a rap artist who by mistake is invited to Tehran to conduct an orchestra. The twist in their humor is that sinners are kinder than the righteous – a theme popular with the great story teller, Jesus.

In fact, many Iranian films have themes which are relevant to Jesus' teaching. For the church, there is an opportunity to reach vast audiences: one good movie could influence millions for Christ.

PRAY FOR CINEMA

◆ *For outstanding Iranian Christian film makers to be raised up and for their films to impact the region.*

◆ *That millions watching Iranian films would be open to the Gospel as they ponder underlying messages.*

◆ *For Iranian film directors and others in the industry to be reached with the Christian message.*

DAY 30 MISSION TO IRAN, ALL CAN PLAY A PART

We can't be missionaries in Iran, but we can all play a part in equipping Christians there to be effective witnesses. This is what successful mission is all about, as the story below shows.

Hassan and his wife Shadi were driving in Tehran at 1:00 am and stopped at a red light. Noticing a man in the car next to them, Shadi said: *"We need to give this man a New Testament."* Hassan jumped out of the car and knocked on the man's window. *"I am a Christian and would like to give you a copy of the Gospel of Christ."* Startled, the man, named Babak, said, *"This morning I said: God, show me how I can know you."*

Some months later, Babak came to Hassan's house and gave his life to Christ. Before leaving, he told Hassan, *"That night we met at the traffic lights I had been following you for twenty minutes, because something told me to."*

Praise God for Hassan and Shadi who were willing to take the risk and share the Word of God.

Praise God for ministries that helped disciple and equip them.

Praise God for Christians worldwide who sent New Testaments to Iran.

Praise God for those who pray for the salvation of people like Babak and intercede for servants like Hassan and Shadi.

The evening that changed Babak's life was not just the work of one Iranian Christian. It was God at work through His people around the world.

PRAY FOR MISSION TO IRAN

◆ *For more believers to be called to reach Iran.*

◆ *For more intercession on behalf of Iran.*

◆ *For the resources needed to strengthen and expand the church.*

So... what next?

If you are being led to serve the Church in Iran, here are some ways to get involved:

1. **Continue praying for Iran.** Visit **www.iran30.org** and sign up to receive monthly prayer requests.

2. **Share this book** with other Christians and churches. Visit **www.iran30.org** and order copies for your friends.

3. **Witness to Iranians**. Visit **www.elam.com/shop where** Persian Scriptures and evangelistic materials are available.

4. **Serve a ministry** working among Iranians. There are short, medium and long-term opportunities.

5. **Send New Testaments to Iran**. Contact Elam for details.

About Elam Ministries

Elam was founded by senior Iranian church leaders with a passion to train and equip Iranian Christians to reach and disciple their countrymen. The ministry began in 1990 when six Iranian Christians arrived in England for Bible training. Since then, Elam has seen many years of God's faithfulness and is now being used to strengthen and expand the church in the Iran region.

Thousands of Iranian Christians have been trained; hundreds of thousands of Scriptures have been distributed; over 150 books have been published in Persian; TV programs are reaching large numbers every week; and churches are being planted in Iran at an increasing rate.

Today Elam is involved with:

· Training leaders and workers for the Iranian church
· Enabling church planting, evangelism and discipleship
· Sending Bibles and resources
· Reaching Iranians through TV and the Internet
· Sending relief for the poor and persecuted

Elam partners with a number of different ministries and organizations to serve the church in the Iran region.

Visit **www.elam.com** for more information or contact us at:

USA office: 5755 North Point Parkway - Suite 217, Alpharetta, GA 30022
UK office: PO Box 75, Godalming, Surrey, GU8 6YP